Author's Statement

The author will use proper medical names for parts of the body. Most cultures use slang terms or euphemisms for organs. However the correct anatomical terms are used to avoid any misunderstanding, and these terms will be explained as they are used.

A 14 year old, unfolds a "mind-field" of questions and answers. The many conflicts she encounters. Her words are heartrending, delicate and innocent. A strange event took place, a visual illuminating mystery, that envelope into a quiet but secret relationship with Sam. This multi-layered excursion is her story.

This book is written for readers who are 14 years old or older.

Pink Rainbow

by

Dr. O. D. Groves

Cover Design: Dr. O. D. Groves

Published by G Publishing, LLC
P. O. Box 24374
Detroit, MI 48224

ISBN 13:   978-0-9845971-6-1
      10: 0-9845971-6-6

Library of Congress Control Number:
      2012907824

Printed in the United States of America

Acknowledgments

Thank You:

Lillian Blackshire for thoroughly reading the manuscript for publication

About the Book

This book is about ME in my past, as I lived my life! I had a restless appetite for new experiences! During my adolescent years my life was in a turmoil trying to do my own things. I made new friends, went new places and tried new things.

During this stage of my life I lived the way I thought was right, for me, keeping things private and secret, not realizing the consequences I might encounter. As I continue sailing on my imaginary Pink Rainbow, not understanding the changes going on inside of me or around me in the world I made for myself – and the choices that I put in my world, my innocence and lack of knowledge would have been my downfall. I needed answers and understanding of what was going on. The changes were happening too fast, so I had to write them down. I bought a big book to record my situations.

This book would not have been written had it not been for a baffling real or imagined revelation (Sam's writing appearing on the pages) as I longed for answers – a miraculous vision, shocking but real provided written words answers to my many dilemmas. The wisdom I needed as my adolescent years unraveled the mysteries of my developmental stages which were an unbelievable excursion of life; but, I did survive.

Q - My Very Special Mark

I am Quintella Essolene Watson. My friends call me Telli. I am 14 years old and I am in the 9th grade. I have one brother named August, and one sister named Calynn. August is 12 years old and Calynn is 10 years old. My mother is a beautician. Her name is Barbara. I think she's 30 or 40 years old. Every time we use the word "ain't" in a sentence, Mommy takes a nickel from our allowance, and puts the nickels in big jar. The jar got plenty nickels in it, mostly mine and August.

Mrs. Wilson, the lady next door, comes over to watch over us when mommy leaves. I am old enough to take care of August and Calynn, and me. Mrs. Wilson helps me pop — popcorn, and stuff. When we watch a movie on T.V. sometimes, August and Calynn usually fall asleep. Since I am going to be a writer when I grow up, I watch the movies so I can write about what happens and all to people.

I have special friends at school, but my best friend is Rita Sloan. We all eat lunch together; go to the mall together, and things and stuff like that. I have a boyfriend. His name is

Chucky. He is 14 ½ years old. He has red hair. That's my favorite color, that's why I picked him. But I need someone I can really talk to. My friends don't know everything, like private stuff and all, and super cool stuff.

One of these days, I am going to get me a big book <u>that's it</u> so I can write private stuff in. Like I said, I don't want anybody to read it but me. My book is going to be awesome and supper cool.

Q

Dr. O. D. Groves

My

Private

Book

"Sam"

_Q_

This is my first time writing in my private book. I am 14 years old, and old enough to make my own decisions, (people always telling me what to do, and other private things.) That's why I need you to talk to about my private things.

Q

You are entering the most formative years of your development 14 years and adding...The decisions you make now, will affect you the rest of your like. Choose wisely, consult someone you can trust and surround yourself with people that are on your side. Remember, people who are on your side!

Sam

I almost threw the book on the floor—I couldn't believe what I saw, writing on the page like magic or something. The writing gave me the "heevie geevies" ----should I tell my mother? Should I tell my friends? Maybe I will tell my teacher? ... Mrs. Alberti will understand....Should I tell somebody? No! No! No! I'm going to keep it a "secret".---My secret and Sam's...I will hide Sam someplace. Wow! Wow! That was some writing though. I am closing this book. This kind of stuff is crazy. I think.

Q

S
M
O
K
I
N
G

Dr. O. D. Groves

Dear Sam,

Today is the first day back to school. I'm so glad to be in the 9th grade since I finally turned 14 years old. My best friend Rita had a package of cigarettes. She gave me three. I don't know how to smoke. My mother and her friends smoke, but I don't like the smell. Maybe I will try to smoke one...maybe -- since I'm 14.

Q

The warning cn a pack of cigarettes says that cigarette smoke contains "carbon monoxide"; also smoking causes heart disease, emphysema, and lung and mouth cancer.

Your lifestyle requires a lot of movements, exercises, playing with your friends. Your lungs must be free to perform these activities. Cigarette smoke that is drawn into the mouth over a period of time can damage the taste buds, as well as the smelling cells in the nose. Bronchitis may also result from smoking. The decision to smoke or not to smoke is one of the most important decisions you will ever make.

Sam

Dr. O. D. Groves

M (Period Time)

E

N

S

T

R

U

A

T

I

O

N

Dear Sam,

How do you write like that, talking to me on paper? It's sorta weird, new and strange. The way it is going down and all. I don't understand it all, but it is our secret. I'm still trying to find you a good hiding place. I will soon.

I don't feel too well today. I have cramps. I don't like this 'period stuff' don't have the hang of it yet. When I started bleeding down there, I thought I had cut myself. I was eleven then. I told my mother and stuff. She told me about boys and things, and babies and sex and all. It was all—just stuff, didn't make sense to me.

Sam, sometimes my friends talk about this period stuff, never with the boys though. I told you about my boy friend. His name is Charles. He is fourteen and a-half years old. He was named after his father, so everybody calls him Chucky, me too.   We all play together. I mean, me and my girl friends and their boy friends.

Let's get back to this period stuff. My mother gives me a box of "sanitary napkins" every month to wear. Oh I felt horrible then the first time I put them on. I am feeling just horrible now.

Q

The menstruation period is a cycle that occurs every 27 or 28 days, and releases material from your body you didn't use. You are leaving childhood and entering a stage of physical and sexual maturity. Oh, tampons are used also, (a choice girls make).

Sam

Sam, why do I have to bleed and all? Is this a baby coming out of me?

Chucky kissed me, and he told me to touch his private. I did.

Q

No, of course not, Telli, you are growing up. The menstrual period is a process when an egg is released from one of your two ovaries, the egg (or ovum) moves down the fallopian tube. If sperm are in the fallopian tube (a process of having sex with a boy) one of them may fertilize the egg.

If the egg is not fertilized, it disintegrates into the "uterus". The lining of the uterus breaks down and comes out of your body as menstrual blood. The bleeding lasts about five (5) days. The lining of the uterus is not needed, because no egg has been fertilized to make a baby. (Remember the egg and ovum are the same.)

Most girls' periods usually follow a regular pattern each month. Sometimes you may skip a month, which is normal. Although being sexually active with a boy or boys usually will produce a baby. This is the stage you have arrived to become a young mother. This is a very important decision you must make!!!, if you are approached to have "sex" (intercourse). <u>The decision you make will control and affect you the rest of your life.</u>

Sam

F

R

I

E

N

D

S

H

I

P

Dr. O. D. Groves

Rita is my best friend. We have been friends since the third grade. We have other friends also. We go to the mall and other places. Rita has a boy friend too. His name is Ron. He is fourteen years old. Sometimes Rita and Ron and Chucky and me go places together. I think Ron gave Rita these cigarettes, I am not sure, but Ron smokes; Chucky don't smoke. I'm glad---cigarettes "<u>stinks</u>" the smoke I mean. They cost too much money too. Chucky don't have much money, me either.

Q

Maybe I can assume you will not become a "smoker"; a nice healthy decision for a fourteen year old girl to make. You don't look cool, either when you smoke.

Sam

Dear Sam,

Rita called me today remember my best friend, and she was crying. You know what she told me? She hadn't seen her period in two months---She told me she had did the "Freaky" with Ron. She said Ron told her how she would not have a baby. "I asked her what did she do to keep from having a baby." She said Ron said if they stood up while during the "Freaky", she would not get pregnant, and she should take a bath as soon as she get home. These two things works every time to give you perfect protection from getting a baby. Rita told me she did all of those things, and she wanted to know what should she do now? I told her, I don't know, maybe she should tell someone, her mother or something.

Q

Dr. O. D. Groves

Yes, Rita should tell someone, to be sure what is exactly happening to her. In the meanwhile, check the Information Bank on <u>Conception and Contraception.</u>

Sam

YOU

T

E

L

L

I

YOU

Dr. O. D. Groves

Dear Telli,

You are your best friend or your worst enemy—YOU! Welcome to your puberty years during this period of "ADOLESCENCE". Set your mind and body to engage in various changes—Many rapid changes—will take place. Adolescence years are the most exciting time of your life! A "girl" – becomes a "woman"!

Telli, you first must become you, this does take time, but you should be ready. You are fast – becoming a teenager. Your body is to carry out different functions until it reaches physical and mental maturity. Let's begin:

It is necessary to sleep and rest, to eat an adequate diet, and to engage in play through exercise. You must develop habits of cleanliness, and good grooming. Remember to take responsibility for your own actions; such matters as having sex, the use of tobacco, and the use of drugs and alcohol.

You must take responsibility for your own safety, and that of others; such as fires in the home, medical emergencies, strangers entering the home, etc. You must decide what is right or wrong—and if it is—what you believe in, no matter what others are doing or thinking.

Look in the Information Bank on "House Fire"

Sam

Dr. O. D. Groves

S

E

L

F

E

S

T

E

E

M

Self-esteem is merely knowing who you are, knowing those special values you deem important to you only, and feeling good about the decisions you make in life, and what is best for you. Do not be afraid to say "No", if that is the way you feel about a situation and don't feel guilty.

I know you have your father's ears and your mother's pretty eyes and your grandmother's nose. Of course you have features passed down through the genes, but you are an individual with your unique qualities with a little cultivating you will come out okay.

Your parents have taught you right and wrong, and how to get along with other people. Your family, friends, are the most influential people in your life, but don't forget you. You have become aware that there are other people having different ideas, and may probably

Dr. O. D. Groves

influence the way you think too. Remember, you have a mind of your own. It's up to you which values you take from friends, and family—and which values you will reject. This is a process of growing up!

Telli, you may think you are "ugly" cosmetics hold the answer for you – you will probably try these things to look your best. Remember you are not a "model," having lights and makeup and professional tricks to make you look a certain way. As you grow, many changes will occur. You may have pimples on your face. Your hair may be oilier. You may look taller as you lose that baby fat. This will all change in time, and in your favor of looking better.

Your lifestyle is very important in determining your shape. In order to burn calories, you must exercise. The extra pounds we gain will be stored in the body as fat. Exercising or being active will burn these calories. So get moving, with your friends. Develop bodies that are beautiful and healthy.

Sam

Dr. O. D. Groves

B
U
L
L
Y
I
N
G

Dear Sam:

This girl likes my boy friend; but Chucky said he didn't like her. When she sees me alone at school, she says nasty things to me, and she is going to beat me up; she and her friends. I ain't (oops, I owe Mommy a nickel) scared of her, but I don't like fighting either.

Q

Bullying is child abuse by children. If someone is bullying you, report it immediately to your parents and school officials. These hateful messages and intimidations could escalate to assault, rape or murder. With the advent of social networking sites and cell phones, bullies are now able to spread their hurtful messages to the masses, and the effects are devastating. Bullying has become a major problem in our

Dr. O. D. Groves

schools, and society. It's sad, but it is a reality.

Fight or not to fight----. Fighting with someone may damage your body over a situation that could have been settled in another way. Using your head, may be best for everyone involved. You will look prettier too afterward.

Sam

E

A

T

I

N

G

Dr. O. D. Groves

Sam:

My friends made fun of a fat girl today. The girl started crying. I <u>ain't*</u> never going to be fat, cause I'm not going to eat breakfast--- and school lunches anymore. That ought to keep me little.

*Another nickel for the jar.

Q

Telli, the body must have food to function properly. It so happens your food intake is not controlled by you. Your mother insists you eat breakfast and dinner at home, and she does purchase snacks, such as fruits and yogurt to eat as snacks. Here are a few rules you may follow. These are the nutrients you need; remember, going on crash diets or starving yourself is unhealthy and dangerous. Now, let's begin:

Protein Carbohydrates and Fats.

Protein such as meat is used by the body to form cell tissues that help you grow. Fish, nuts, eggs, cheese, and beans all contain large amounts of protein.

Carbohydrates provide fuel for the body. You need the energy to live, work, and play. Carbohydrates are found in breads, potatoes, cereals, rice, beans and pasta. Sugars are carbohydrates too, which occur in fruits and many vegetables and milk.

Fats give you energy just as carbohydrates, they also help build cells. Fats are easily recognizable. You find them in cooking oil, butter, and margarine. There are other foods which have high fat content, such as nuts, cookies, sausages and cheese.

Dr. O. D. Groves

As a teenager you need a balanced diet. You must eat in order to live, and that will be the rest of your life. Get food charts. The internet provides valuable information you will need as you grow. Choose wisely; learn about fiber, vitamins, sugar in disguise, and mineral magic.

Vegetarians: There are five types of vegetarians:

1. Ovo-acto-vegetarians
2. Lacto-vegetarians
3. Ovo-vegetarians
4. Fruitarians
5. Vegans

Vegetarians must also make an effort to get vitamins and minerals.

Food Allergies: Many people suffer from allergies, when the body reacts unusually with certain foods and is sensitive to certain foods. Children often outgrow some allergies, others persists into adulthood.

Food Additives: Food additives are many substances deliberately added to food during its preparation.

Processed Foods: Refers to any change made to basic foods, or making a new food.

Organic Produce: Refers to growing foods on natural substance with no chemical spraying on the food.

Food Poisoning: Results from eating food that is poisonous in itself or contaminated by bacteria or chemicals.

Fast Foods: Fast foods have a bad reputation because fast foods are high in fat and low in fiber, vitamins and minerals. Fast food, also called "junk food", is not good for you. Even worse for you are foods

Dr. O. D. Groves

that provide few nutrients other than calories laden with sugar, salt and fat. These foods include cake, candy, ice cream, cookies, soft drinks and chips.

Fast food can be healthy if you choose wisely, such as a baked potato topped with broccoli or a Chinese stir-fry. A vegetable pizza is full of nutrients, or a sandwich made of whole wheat bread, tuna, and cucumber can be a proper meal.

See Fast Foods and Diabetes in the Information Bank

Drinking water is part of a balanced diet also. This is very important! Tell, water is essential; your life depends on water. People are made up mostly of water. Every part of you must have water to work. Your body needs watery solutions to dissolve and transport nutrients and to carry away waste

products. So drink up! As a teenager you have your work cut out
for you. And to help you keep slim
and healthy, don't forget hand
washing before all meals.

Use water or "hand sanitizer"
which is excellent for this. (Smile)
Don't forget, you owe your mother
two nickels.

Sam

D
R
U
G
S

Sam,

We had to go to the auditorium today. Some people were there talking about drugs. I don't use any drugs. I don't even know what they look like or what they are good for. They said something about using illegal drugs or misusing legal drugs. The talked about medicinal drugs is drugs abuse or something like that.

Q

Telli, it is essential that you know about drugs. So let's get started. My dear little Telli, all medicines are drugs. Medical drugs are a blessing when they are used properly; but, some people use them improperly, especially teen-agers who use them to get high. Don't be pressured into using drugs. Drugs are expensive, and few young people can afford them. Selling or using Illegal drugs can get you into serious trouble with the law. Drug abusers need professional guidance and medical treatments.

Sam

For further information, look in the Information Bank.

Sam, my mother told me to place paper on the toilet seat every time I use a public restroom. You might catch HIV or something.

Q

Telli, for safety reasons no one should sit on a wet toilet seat. Many public restrooms supply paper toilet seat covers. Using them on dry toilet seats provides some protection. As far as HIV is concerned, please consult the Information Bank for further knowledge.

Sam

G
A
Y

(HOMOSEXUALITY)

Dr. O. D. Groves

Sam, there is a boy in my class, and they said he is funny...you know, he don't like girls and all. I think they said he is gay...and he like boys only, or something.

Q

Telli, don't you think you and your friends are too young to be involved in romantic relationships? Most boys are interested only in playing sports with boys. They are not particularly attracted to members of the opposite sex. Some boys don't feel comfortable with girls. These types of friendships are common among boys in this age group. Look in your Information Bank on Homosexuality.

Sam

F
E
E
L
I
N
G
S

AND

E
M
O
T
I
O
N
S

Dr. O. D. Groves

August took my new toothbrush the dentist gave me. I am mad, I am really mad, Sam! August keeps getting into my things; I can't keep anything around him. I want a tattoo, most girls have one. Mommy said just plain "NO", case closed. I lost my glove at school. Rita went to the mall today with another friend; they didn't ask me, we always go together. My mother wouldn't let me go to the park to play. Instead I had to help her. This is not my day!

I was accused for something I didn't do...by another student. It's not <u>fair</u>. All my friends have their ears pierced. My mother won't let me; she wants me to wait. She wants her friend who is a nurse to pierce my ears when I am fifteen. I want them pierced now. Calynn found my makeup box, and took my lipstick out of it and lost it. I have to find another hiding place. "I can't do anything that I want to do.

All my friends wear pretty hanging earrings; they look sharp." My friend knows a lady that can pierce my ears for two dollars. I'm saving my money. I'm going to have my ears pierced. I saw the earrings I want today. Here, look in today's newspaper, these are the earrings I want, they are the most.

Q

When your mother told you specifically not to do something, there must have been a good reason for this, don't you think?

Consult the Information Bank on "Ears".

Telli, Telli, it would be easy to place a band aid over the hurt parts and all would be well again. Life does not work like that, but here's something that should help you, for example: Everyone has feelings or emotions. We all get angry, have hurt feelings, and are sad, fearful and unhappy. You set your standards how you expect people to respond or react to you. This includes your friends, parents, siblings or anyone else that crosses your path. You must learn to manage your emotions in ways that help you and do not hurt others or yourself.

This will aid you to be a strong and healthy person. When you feel that others are leaving you out of things or do not want you around, remember that you may be mistaken in thinking people feel this way about you too. So instead of keeping off by yourself, try making some friendly moves of your own. You can make friends with others outside of your special group who seem unfriendly to you. Remember too, that people do not like all of their acquaintances well enough to want to be special friends with them.

Some people in authority will take advantage of their position and criticize you to be purely spiteful. Tell your parent or an adult that you trust. You don't have to put up with this type of criticism.

If you frequently feel quarrelsome, stop and ask yourself, "Is it because you always want to have your own way?" If so, try giving in now and then. If you give others their way at times, you will find that they are more likely to go along with you and let you have your way at other times. Think back to be sure you have not misunderstood another person's words or actions.

Temporarily turn your thoughts away from your upset feelings until you feel calm and better able to deal with them. Try to do something for others, take part in some strenuous activity, look for a good TV program or get active.

Sam

S

E

X

Dr. O. D. Groves

Dear Sam,

I am really confused and mired up. Chucky ask me to do the "freaky", he want us to make love. He showed me some funny looking rubber thing his brother gave him that keeps me from having a baby. Chucky still lets me touch his private thing, when we hug and kiss and all. I told him I would think about it. I am not quite ready yet. I am not sure if this is what I want to do.

Q

The decision to have a sexual relationship is an important one. Feelings of attraction to someone are exciting. You may be nervous. As a teenager, you are curious about sex. At the same time, many teenagers feel that the sex education they receive at school is not private or personal enough. Their friends' information is not accurate

and can be harmful. Many teenagers find it hard to talk to their
parents or other adults.

These days the decision to become
sexually active must also take into
account the spread of AIDS and
other sexually transmitted diseases
(STDs). If you are even vaguely
scared or uncertain say "no".
Before you decide to become
sexually active you need to answer
this important question in your
own mind: Is this what you really
want to do, or are you being
pressured by Chucky and your
friends?

There is however, a correct
decision for you. This is a major
decision and an important part of
your life. Don't cheat yourself!

Sam

S A M ' s
INFORMATION

B
A
N
K

CONTENTS:
Contraception (Birth Control)
Conception
Drugs
Ear Piercing and Tattooing
Fast Food and Diabetes
Hand Washing
HIV
House Fire
Homosexuality
Sun

CONTRACEPTION

Contraceptives are methods of birth control. Many young people start by using condoms because they are inexpensive, convenient and easy to use.

<u>Male Condom</u> – a very thin sheath, usually made of latex rubber, put on the man's erect penis before intercourse.

<u>Female Condom</u> – a soft polyurethane bag placed inside the vagina. It is held in place by an inner ring with an outer ring that lies over the area outside the vagina.

<u>Diaphragm</u> – a soft rubber dome that fits over the cervix. Before intercourse, the woman coats that diaphragm with a spermicide and inserts it into the vagina. She must leave it in place for at least six hours.

Dr. O. D. Groves

Birth Control Pill – usually just called "the pill". The woman takes a series of pills every month. The pill provides highly effective protection against pregnancy if the woman diligently takes the series of pills.

CONCEPTION

Two kinds of cells are needed to become pregnant or to have a baby, an Ovum or egg from the girl's body and a Sperm from the boy's body. A boy and a girl make a baby when the boy's sperm fertilizes the girl's Ovum or egg. The two cells meet when the boy ejaculates (an abrupt discharge of fluid, called semen) into the girl's vagina during the act of having Sex (sexual intercourse).

Once sperm are ejaculated into the vagina, they wriggle their long threadlike tail and swim up through the cervix and into the uterus on their way up into the fallopian tubes. Although millions of sperm are ejaculated into the girl's vagina, only a few thousand get this far (the rest die absorbed by the girl's body).

One sperm may pass through the Ovum's outer barrier and fuse with it to form one new cell. Only one sperm can unite with the egg or Ovum. When the egg is fertilized by this one sperm, the egg then travels down the fallopian tube and begins to divide again and again to form a small ball of cells.

The soft thickened lining of the uterus is now needed, so hormones are produced that prevent it from breaking down and being shed. Therefore, no menstrual period will occur. Instead, during the second week after conception (fertilization) the tiny ball of cells implants itself in the blood enriched lining of the uterus. The tiny ball of cells taps into

Dr. O. D. Groves

the girl's (its mother) blood supply and starts to grow into a baby.

DRUGS

Amphetamines – commonly known as speed, uppers, yellow crystal or powder. Obtained in pills or capsules can be sniffed or injected.

Cannabis – street names are marijuana, pot, dope, hash and grass, is a resinous material or leafy herbal mixture. It is smoked in a joint or pipe.

Cocaine – also known as coke, blow, snow, is a white powder commonly sniffed; but can be injected or some-times smoked. Crack Cocaine is an especially dangerous highly addictive form of cocaine. Even in small amounts, cocaine can cause sudden death in young people. If someone accidently overdoses, he or she may become unconscious or even die.

Heroin – also known as smack, scag, H, or horse is a white or brown powder that can be sniffed, injected or smoked.

LSD – (Acid) tablet and small paper or gelatin squares is taken by mouth. Its effects are unpredictable and range from excitement to panic, fear, and hallucination.

Mescaline – (Peyote) is a hallucinogenic drug obtained from certain forms of cactus, usually smoked or eaten.

Psilocybin – (Magic Mushroom) is a type of mushroom containing a substance similar to LSD. It produces hilarity, over excitement, and with high doses dream-like images.

Barbiturates and Tranquilizers – also known as downers, reds and other prescribed tablets. Prescribed tablets and capsules are sometimes taken illegally. They are similar in effect to alcohol and the effects are increased when taken with alcohol.

Inhalants – Sniffing and breathing in chemicals found in household cleaning products as well as aerosols, glues, thinners and gasses. Inhalants are addictive and accidental overdoses are common and can result in death.

EAR PIERCING AND TATTOOING

Pierced Ears – People with pierced ears have a tiny hole in the earlobe. You can have your ears pierced by a jeweler, a doctor, or a nurse. If sterile equipment is not used, the ear tissue is easily infected. A needle that has been used before and had been exposed to hepatitis or the AIDS virus could transfer these infections to the healthy ear. If an infection develops and won't go away, seek medical attention immediately.

After your ears are pierced you should wear gold or stainless steel earrings. Some people are allergic to certain metals. If so, they should continue to wear only hypoallergenic earrings. Hypoallergenic means having little likelihood of causing an allergic response. You should read the label on the card when purchasing earrings.

Different kinds of earrings

-	Post earrings have a thin shaft that is attached and goes through the earlobe hole and is secured with a butterfly clip or other type clip.
-	Hooked earrings have a thin wire hook that passes through the earlobe hole.
-	Clip-On earrings are fastened to the ear with a clip that gently pinches the earlobe.

Dr. O. D. Groves

Tattooing or any type of body piercings including ear piercing, are risk taking activities. All materials used for these procedures should be sanitized and uncontaminated. Hepatitis C can be transmitted through a dirty needle.

Hepatitis C is a contagious liver disease that is caused by the Hepatitis C Virus (HCV). If people want a tattoo, they must make sure the establishment is licensed. Once (HCV) is in the blood stream if does not go away.

FAST FOODS AND DIABETES

Diabetes is a growing disease in your age group due in large part to making poor choices in selecting foods at "Fast Food" restaurants. Eating food such as carbohydrates that have too many calories, and not exercising contributes to poor bone building, lack of muscle power, gaining weight and developing diabetes, heart and circulatory problems. The heart thrives on exercises; make the heart strong!

Teenagers usually eat a diet high in animal fats which produces fat and cholesterol in their blood. They are on their way to having heart disease or strokes later in life. Exercise removes glucose, a form of sugar, from the blood.

Dr. O. D. Groves

HAND WASHING

Wash your hands! Keeping clean is very important, especially washing the hands before eating any food, whether you are at home or away from home. Wash the hands after using the bathroom in your friends' homes or in public restrooms. Washing the hands also helps control infectious viruses that cause the common cold. Wash your hands before preparing food or serving food. You may also use a hand sanitizer which comes in a bottle that you can carry in your purse.

HIV -
HIV and AIDS

Telli, many people believe that HIV is the same as AIDS, but it is not. HIV is the name given to the virus that causes the disorder called AIDS. If someone has been exposed to HIV, the body produces antibodies to fight the virus. So if a blood test shows that these antibodies are present, the person has been infected with HIV. This condition is referred to as being HIV positive.

AIDS – stands for "acquired immuno-deficiency syndrome". AIDS is not an illness in itself. It is any one of a number of illnesses that can occur in a person with HIV infection who has very poor immunity.

Medical authorities agree that HIV does not survive well in the environment, making the possibility of environmental transmission remote. In order for HIV to be transmitted: (1) HIV must be present and (2) HIV must get inside the body. HIV has been known to survive in drug injector syringes since these are airtight and contain blood from the injected.

Dr. O. D. Groves

Sexual behavior that can transmit HIV: Vaginal Sex (penis in the vagina), Anal Sex (penis in the anus) involving either men or women; Oral Sex (mouth on the penis or vagina).

The risk of transmitting HIV is greatly reduced by using a condom. It is important to remember that HIV is not transmitted through saliva, tears, sweat, feces or urine, hugging, kissing, massages, shaking hands, insect bites, living in the same house with someone who has HIV, sharing showers or toilets with someone with HIV.

HOUSE FIRE

If you discover a fire in your house, alert your family at once. Then everyone should leave the house, even if the fire seems small. Once a fire is started, it grows with frightening speed. The fire department can be called from a neighbor's home, or a family's cell phone. Do not hang up until you are sure the message has been correctly understood.

HOMOSEXUALITY

Homosexuality is a very sensitive issue, and it is ironic that people judge people merely by eye observation in determining their sexual orientation. These statements are piercing and sometimes have a crippling effect on the person so labeled. There are various concepts as to why people are said to be homosexual or gay.

During one of the stages of development, some teenagers choose to interact with peers of the same gender. It is viewed by some, that this stage of development is the final period of shaping one's sexual identity. This conclusion becomes the greatest threat of a teenager's sexual security, and the rejection of these teenagers begins to take form.

Some are harassed by name calling and homosexual slurs; such as sissies, queers, or being effeminate and gay. These teenagers are labeled by their peers and sometimes by their elders. The comments which are embarrassing, distressing, cruel and detrimental are made with no thought of the teenager's feelings. It is believed that these events are the beginning of ostracism by their family, peers and other group relationships.

Let's consider a few scenarios that are held very firmly: (1) a male teenager that displays effeminate behavior patterns may be labeled as being a homosexual; (2) however, a female teenager who does not display utter feminine patterns is called a tomboy, but poses no concern to society, and she is not labeled or called lesbian or gay, which seemly is a standard of acceptability by most.

Some teenagers have long term future career plans that they may pursue. However, interacting with the opposite sex, especially in a sexual relationship may prevent them from careers as doctors or other chosen careers which require substantial education.

Some teenagers grow up in dys-functional environments or family systems that are not an acceptable code of behavior:

-domestic violence

-sexual abusiveness

-alcoholism and drug use,

-rape

-incest

Dr. O. D. Groves

-too many teenagers with parental responsibilities

These conditions have a tendency for some teenagers to remain celibate or to conduct limited or no involvement with the opposite sex, thereby causing them to be labeled as homosexuals.

After teenagers reach their most formative years on leaving the childhood stage and enter puberty, many changes occur; boys become men and girls become women. During the puberty period of development a child becomes an adult capable of sexual reproduction, i.e., fathering or bearing a child.

During this period of adolescence teenagers are no longer thought of as "kids". The puberty years are the years of change, changing standards of acceptability by society.

SUN
MR. SUN AND YOUR SKIN

Teenagers spend a lot of time outdoors, especially on the beach during summer...riding their bikes, playing ball or other activities. Moderate sun exposure helps teen-agers to produce vitamin D, which activates the calcium needed for growing strong bones.

Black or brown-skinned teenagers are somewhat protected from the high rays of sun by the melamine in their skin. Overexposure to the sun by fair—skinned teenagers can be dangerous, causing severe sunburn and other skin disorders.

Dr. O. D. Groves

Why "A Pink Rainbow", Telli?

It is common knowledge that a "Rainbow" has seven colors:

1. Red
2. Orange
3. Yellow
4. Green
5. Blue
6. Indigo (a dark violet blue)
7. Violet

You chose the color "Pink", why?

Sam

Because I am a girl, Sam and pink is a girl's color. I want the world to see me as I am, a "girl" sailing on my Pink "Rainbow".

Q

Sam, what do you look like? Are you cute and stuff?

Q

Are looks that important, Telli?
Here is a picture of me.

Sam

Dr. O. D. Groves

About the Author

O. D. Groves has a B.S., a M.S., and an Ed.D.

- Doctor of Education

- Phi Delta Kappa member

- A member of the Society of Children's Book Writers and Illustrators

- Author of ten books

- Marquis's Who's Who in America "2008"

CPSIA information can be obtained at www.ICGtesting.com
Printed in the USA
BVOW040133220512

290761BV00001B/3/P